How to Enjoy Supernatural Prosperity

Lowell Lundstrom

HARVEST HOUSE PUBLISHERS
Irvine, California 92714

HOW TO ENJOY SUPERNATURAL PROSPERITY

Copyright © 1979 by Lowell Lundstrom

Published by Harvest House Publishers Irvine, California 92714

Library of Congress Catalog Card Number 79-87771
ISBN 0-89081-204-7

Printed in the United States of America.

Contents

Chapter 1
HOW TO KNOW WHAT YOU'RE LOOKING FOR

Money!
Prosperity!
Success!
The newstands are lined with magazines and the bookstores are filled with books about these subjects. Schools and colleges include special classes in their schedules, motivational groups conduct "how to" seminars and clinics, and promoters offer investment schemes and business opportunities that propose to catapult you to the top. Even certain religious groups have developed "blessing plans" which they claim will produce nearly-instant prosperity for those who use them.

I've read a lot of these books and magazines, and I've talked with lots of people about the most popular success and prosperity programs. Some of the programs I found interesting and worthwhile, but others were either foolish or outright rip-offs. Some of the religious approaches are based on Scripture, while others are based on mistaken interpretations.

Frankly, I have always been leery of the "pray-and-get-rich" schemes. My conviction is that we should love God for who He is, with no strings attached. Trying to bargain with God for financial gain or attempting to manipulate the promises of the Bible into some kind of spiritual stock market will lead to sure disappointment.

The Bible warns us to beware of men who have "corrupt minds, destitute of truth, supposing that gain is godliness: from such withdraw thyself" (1 Timothy 6:5).

God Says a Lot About Money

The Word of God has much to say about material prosperity. Jesus spoke 35 parables that are recorded in the Gospels. Of these, more than a third deal directly with the subject of money and possessions. As a matter of fact, one out of every five verses in the Bible has something to say about money, wealth, or possessions. And contrary to what some people think, God isn't against riches and wealth. Time and again we are told that God rewarded righteous men with material increase as well as with spiritual blessings.

The story of Job is a classic example. After all his trials, after all his sufferings, after all his heartaches and griefs, God restored to Job everything that had been taken away. In fact, the Bible says, "The Lord gave Job twice as much as he had before" (Job 42:10).

And 2 Chronicles 26:5 describes the reign of King Uzziah of Judah by saying, "As long as he sought the Lord, God made him to prosper."

So I want to emphasize that I do not agree with people who feel that success, money, prosperity, and material things are somehow bad in themselves. There is absolutely nothing in Scripture to support the belief that true spirituality cannot exist amid material prosperity—that poverty and piety are somehow synonymous. This common mistake is too often accepted as truth. People can go to hell in a hovel as readily as in a castle!

On the other hand, many people make the mistake of thinking that money can buy happiness. Within most of us is buried the idea that more money equals more happiness. How did this idea get there? Modern advertising has a lot to do with it. Skillful promotional programs are designed to convince and persuade—to create within the consumer a desire to buy, invest, own, or improve something. Part of the fantasy created by advertising is the belief that quantity equals quality . . . that more is better . . . that happiness is a direct result of how much you accumulate. But that just isn't true.

Tires and Bikes

I remember when I learned the hard lesson that *things* alone do not produce happiness. I was just a boy at the time.

I'll never forget the fun we used to have rolling tires. We would get a few 6:00 X 16 tires and spend the day rolling them around town. I was happy until the day one of my buddies went speeding past me on a bicycle.

As I saw him flying by, a feeling of jealousy rose up in me. I thought, "Look at that lucky guy! He has a bike and all I have is this old tire!" I wasn't happy rolling tires anymore. That night I rushed home, found a Sears catalog, and spent the rest of the evening trying to persuade my father to buy me a bike.

I worked hard that summer and saved my money. I earned about half the amount I needed, and then one Saturday Dad helped me buy the bike I had been saving for. I'll never forget how happy I was riding my new bike to school the next Monday. The kids gathered around and I explained all the special features of my new set of wheels. I was happy! But as I look back on it now, I realize I wasn't any happier with the bike than I had been with the tire.

Bikes and Horses

Things went along great for a while. We must have ridden our bicycles hundreds of miles that summer. Then one day a friend went riding by on a horse! I had been listening to the Lone Ranger on radio, and the thrill of the wild West was in my blood. The sight of my friend flying by on a white horse threw me into depression again. I thought, "Look at that lucky guy! He rides with ease and I have to pedal this old bike like the devil." That night I was begging my father to buy me a horse.

I thought I'd never get a horse, but one morning when Dad awakened me I could tell by the look in his eye that there was something good outside, and it had four legs and a tail. I raced from my bedroom down the stairway—and just outside the door was a beautiful buckskin mare. Wow! I couldn't wait to ride it.

I'll never forget the thrill of taking an evening ride on Smokey. As the horse raced along the trail I could almost hear the music of the Lone Ranger, the William Tell Overture, playing in the background. But as I look back on it now, I wasn't any happier with the horse than I had been with the bike . . . or than I had been with the tire.

Horses and Cars

One day I was riding my horse along the road when "Whooosh"— a friend of mine went speeding by in a yellow Ford convertible. My heart sank again. I thought, "Look at that lucky guy! There he goes in a cloud of dust and all I have is this old nag." I wasn't happy with my horse anymore—I wanted to get a car and girlfriend like the rest of the older guys.

I saved my money, and with the help of a loan from the Bank of Sisseton, I went to Minneapolis to buy a car. My father sent me to a mechanic friend of his for advice so I wouldn't buy a lemon. We searched for a good car without success. Finally the mechanic sold me his personal car. It was a green Buick with an automatic transmission. That transmission was so slow that you could throw it in gear, go in and have lunch, and still come out in time to drive it away! I remember heading home from the Twin cities— happy and proud because now I had my own car. When I arrived home, the fuel gauge reminded me I had my own gas bill, too!

As I look back on it now, I realize I wasn't any happier with the car than I had been with a tire to roll down the street. Even then it began to dawn on me that happiness was not found in things. Jesus said, "A man's life consisteth not in the abundance of the things which he possesseth" (Luke 12:15).

The High Price of Possessions

But many people still don't understand this fact. H.A. Overstreet, author of *Mature Mind*, said, "Men are miserable because they desire things, and because desire can never be wholly satisfied."

Consider people who seek happiness in material things. Many people work overtime and moonlight on a second job to pick up extra money for luxuries. For many families, home has become a refueling station and a hotel instead of the haven God meant it to be. Many families are so deeply in debt that it will be years before they will be free.

I heard one woman who was struggling with the family budget and came to this conclusion: "If we skip one car payment, and skip one furniture payment, and postpone one house payment, we'll have enough money for the down payment on a new color TV set."

Then I heard about the fellow who went to his psychiatrist and said, "I have one of the most beautiful homes in Hollywood. I have a chauffeured Cadillac, two swimming pools (one for the children), and a helicopter to take me to the beach club. I belong to an exclusive golf club, I own a yacht with a crew of six, and I eat so well that my Diner's Club bill averages more than $1000 a month."

"Under those circumstances," asked the psychiatrist, "What kind of problem could you possibly have?"

"My problem, doctor, is that I only make 50 bucks a month!"

When your outgo exceeds your income, your upkeep will be your downfall. Hopefully not many people have this poor fellow's problem. But the fact is that most families spend more than they earn, and keep on doing so until their debts become more than they know how to control. The U.S. Bureau of Labor Statistics in a recent survey of more than 10,000 families in 91 cities discovered that the average family spends $400 more each year than it earns!

And that causes problems. The Ladies' Home Journal reports that over 70 percent of our modern worries are about money. A national association of family counselors estimates that 90 percent of divorces are finance-related.

God did not intend life to be like this! While His Word clearly indicates that we should not be preoccupied with possessions and wealth, the

Bible also declares that God will supply all our needs.

There are some Christians who have applied God's laws to their spiritual needs but have never discovered or obeyed the laws of God that govern their material prosperity.

God Wants You to Prosper

God has established laws that determine your financial destiny just as He has established laws that determine your spiritual destiny. To say that God cares about your spirit and soul but doesn't care about your physical and material needs is false. The Bible teaches that your body is the temple of the Holy Spirit. Jesus did not abandon the multitudes on the hillsides after they listened to His Sermon the the Mount. Instead, He fed them by multiplying the loaves and fishes from the little boy's lunch.

Don't be misled by thinking there is something wrong with a desire to suceed financially. There are at least 1000 passages that speak about personal prosperity. In passages where the Bible criticized rich men, the context showed that it was not their money but their *undue love for money* that was wrong.

Prosperity Is a Positive Witness

It is not true that piety and poverty always go

together. Look at the examples of such men as Abraham, Isaac, Jacob, Joseph, David, Solomon, Daniel, Joseph of Arimathea, and Cornelius. These men were rich—some of them extremely wealthy—yet they were true, devoted followers of God.

I am not saying that all true Christians are materially rich. Some of the most dedicated Christians I have met over the years have had very little of this world's wealth, but they were so rich spiritually that it was a joy to be with them. However, I have also met dedicated Christians who were very rich as a result of their obedience to God's principles of prosperity.

Both Kinds of Prosperity

After much thought, prayer, and study, I have come to believe that there are both natural and spiritual laws for prosperity. Observing *either* set of laws can produce a measure of material prosperity for an individual. But to be truly rich—to enjoy the full measure of God's divine plan for us—requires obedience to *both* the natural and spiritual laws of prosperity. This results in what I call *supernatural prosperity.* And this is God's perfect will for our lives.

When you study (as I have) the dozens of secular books on success, you will find that most of them give only the worldy viewpoint. They fail to give you the spiritual guidelines for success. The principles they teach are sound; they will work—to a point.

You can learn how to manipulate yourself to the top of the career pile. You can climb the greasy pole of professional advancement. Napolean Hill can teach you how to "Think and Grow Rich." Art Linkletter can tell you "How to Become a Super Salesman." Dale Carnegie can tell you "How to Win Friends and Influence People."

Success magazines are filled with fantastic stories of ordinary men who have discovered the keys to prosperity. In sharing their advice on how to achieve wealth, health, and happiness, they tell you to never give up, to think positive thoughts, to maintain a positive mental attitude, to program your time, and to set life goals. These are all good principles. We should be eager to learn and apply them to our lives. God says His children can learn certain things from the wisdom of the world. Jesus said, "The children of this world are in their generation wiser than the children of light" (Luke 16:8).

Supernatural Prosperity

But there must be something more. Only God

can make it possible for you to enjoy *supernatural prosperity*. His plan of success and prosperity is so simple and beautiful that it can revolutionize your life. This plan is not a carnal method produced through unspiritual means, nor is it an unrealistic promise of pie-in-the-sky when you die. Instead, it is a spiritual plan brought about by the Spirit of God that takes full notice of certain natural laws of life.

You will experience a new dimension in your life when you apply God's principles with faith! This is within reach of any Christian who will pay the price, for God is no respecter of persons. God's natural laws and principles will also work for the non-Christian. Isn't that a shocker? Unbelievers seldom realize that much of their effectiveness is due to the application of God's principles in the natural realm. The lives of men like Henry Ford, Andrew Carnegie, Thomas Edison, Charles Steinmetz, and Leonardo da Vinci were incredibly prolific. God's laws of nature, productivity, resourcefulness, and integrity worked spectacularly for them as well as for many people today.

But while unbelievers may achieve *material* prosperity apart from God, they can never achieve soul satisfaction. Riches gained apart from God are a snare and bring little peace. But *supernatural prosperity* brings an abundance of good that will bless you materially, physically, emotionally, and spiritually.

Observe Both the Spiritual and Natural Laws of Prosperity

There are many religious prosperity plans around, and many of them are based on Biblical truths. The problem with these "blessing" plans is that they fail to observe and incorporate the basic *natural laws of prosperity* that are essential to lasting success.

The word "success" is used only once in all the Bible, but that one time is a clear-cut, decisive revelation of what we must do to achieve supernatural prosperity. This is what God said to His people as they prepared to enter the Promised Land: "This book of the law shall not depart out of thy mouth, but thou shalt meditate therein day and night, that thou mayest observe to do according to all that is written therein; for then thou shalt make thy way prosperous, *and then thou shalt have good success*" (Joshua 1:8).

This book is designed to help you observe the words written in both God's *spiritual* and *natural* laws, so that you may be prosperous and successful. In the following chapters we will talk about the natural laws for success, which I believe are based on good management of your mind, your time, your relationships, and your money.

We will also look into the spiritual laws for success. These laws include recognizing that God owns everything and is the source of all that we receive, and that God promises to reward generous Christian giving.

God expects His children to develop spiritual muscles. The Bible says, "The kingdom of heaven suffereth violence, and the violent take it by force" (Matthew 11:12). Jacob wrestled with the angel of God and said he wouldn't let go until the angel granted his requests. In other words, Jacob insisted on receiving something extra from God. This is the pattern we are to follow. Jesus said that we are to ask, seek, and knock, and not merely be a timid Christian who sits around whining, "If the Lord wants to bless me it will work out all by itself." As obedient children of God, we can claim His blessings with authority, based on His Word.

The Richest Life

When you have learned how to order your life in accordance with God's natural and spiritual laws, you will find yourself enjoying a life that is richer, more fulfilling, and more satisfying than you ever thought possible. That is my prayer for you, and my purpose in writing this book. I can say with the Apostle John, "Beloved, I wish above all things that thou mayest prosper and be in health, even as they soul prospereth" (3 John 2).

Chapter 2
HOW TO BE WISE

A few years ago the news media reported the sensational discovery of a boy who apparently had been reared by wolves.

Authorities theorized that the boy had been lost in the wilderness when he was an infant. Instead of dying from exposure or starvation, the boy may have been adopted by a female wolf which nursed him, protected him, and taught him to survive.

When found, the wolf-boy had long shaggy hair, walked on his hands and knees, and expressed himself in snarls, growls, whimpers, and howls.

Doctors examined the young man and found him to be physically healthy and mentally alert. But because of his long association with the wolves, he thought he was an animal.

Perhaps you think this is a far-out story, and maybe it is. But it is a dramatic illustration of the crucial importance of the relationships we choose in life. The people with whom we surround ourselves determine to a large degree who we are and what we will become. There is much truth in the statement that you can tell a man by the company he keeps.

Manage Your Relationships

Parents soon learn that if they allow their children to play with undisciplined, unruly playmates, their own children soon begin to demonstrate those same bad traits. And if that association is allowed to continue, it will not be long before those "good" children begin to rebel and become just as obnoxious as their playmates.

Strangely enough, these same parents sometimes fail to realize that choosing their own friends and associates is just as important as picking out playmates for their children. As a result, there are multiplied thousands of people going through life saddled with the heavy burdens of doubt, negative thinking, and failure because they chose to spend their time with losers instead of winners.

Have you ever been around a bunch of people who have only bad things to say about everything in general? They don't like the weather—it is either too hot or too cold, too wet or too dry. They don't like what they are served to eat—it is cooked either too much or not enough. They think the country is in bad shape, all politicians are either stupid or crooked, and things are sure to get worse. And pity the poor people who walk by within their view—they are either overdressed and showing off or else hopelessly out-of-style and unaware of the poor impression they are making on others in public.

Have you ever known people like that? How do they make you feel? Chances are that if you're around them long enough you'll find yourself becoming irritable, cranky, and ready to join them in their negative and critical outlook on life.

Good Examples Produce Good Results

Fortunately, the process works the other way around, too. Spend some time around a person who is always cheerful and happy. Listen to his compliments of others, his infectious laugh, and his positive comments about life and the world in general. How does this person influence you?

First, you enjoy being with this friend much more than being with the negative crowd. You find yourself happier and more optimistic. If you stay around him long enough you will probably find yourself patterning your own actions after those you admire most in him.

Perhaps you're wondering if I mean to suggest that the kind of people you associate with can determine whether or not you are prosperous and successful. That's exactly what I mean. You'll never learn how to be successful by hanging around failures all the time. You'll never learn good study and work habits from lazy, slothful friends. You'll never learn thrift and economy from going on shopping sprees with careless, wasteful spenders.

Furthermore, it you persist in associating with this kind of people, you will become like them. There is something to the old folk proverb that says, "Birds of a feather flock together." Cervantes, in his famous play *Don Quixote*, wrote, "Tell me thy company, and I'll tell thee what thou art."

The writer of Proverbs declares, "He that tilleth his land shall have plenty of bread, but he that followeth after vain persons shall have poverty enough" (Proverbs 28:19).

Stick with the Winners

One of the primary natural laws of success is to pick out the key people who can help you become successful in reaching the goals you have set, and then associate with these people. First of all, these people have the power to help you get ahead by giving you instruction, suggestions, and opportunities.

Second, constant association with successful people enables you to observe the way they conduct themselves and to absorb some of their attitudes and outlooks. Soon you begin to mentally envision yourself on that level.

Third, outsiders who see you for the first time tend to evaluate your worth and stature by the quality of your associates.

A word of caution! What I'm talking about is considerably different from attempting to be a social climber or a name-dropper. There is little or no value in basking in the glow of the rich and famous, somehow expecting their light to lift you from obscurity. That will never happen.

But when successful people whom you admire and respect become your companions, and you develop a growing relationship with them, you will soon find yourself being drawn to their level. And soon you will move out yourself—no longer a reflection of others, but an image to be reflectd by others.

The Bible says, "He that walketh with wise men shall be wise." Then the same verse adds a warning: "but a companion of fools shall be destroyed" (Proverbs 13:20).

Losers Produce Losers

A recovered alcoholic once told me, "If I'd

learned earlier in life to associate with the right people rather than with a bunch of drunks, I'd never have ended up as an alcoholic. Now I've learned to cultivate the friendship of the people in Alcoholics Anonymous who can help me stay sober. I didn't join the program as a hobby. I got on the program so I could learn how to get sober and stay sober. I never learned that from any of my drinking buddies."

Dumpy friends make for dumpy success. You must be selective in the friends you keep. This does not mean that you shun others. You should do all you can to help the unfortunate, and you shouldn't feel above them. But it is important to spend most of your time with people who know where they're going. Otherwise you'll find yourself with people who are going nowhere, who are in a rut. And a rut is nothing but a grave with the ends knocked out.

Jesus ministered to everybody, but chose His friends very selectively. He preached and prayed for multitudes, but He had 70 men who were His special disciples. And out of the 70 He had 12 men who formed a closer inner circle. And of those 12 He had three men who were His special friends.

Who your friends are and who you spend your time with *does* make a difference in what happens to you and what you become. I'll never forget a man who came to me after one of our crusade services to tell me his wife was divorcing him. With tears streaming down his face he said, "Lowell, she loved me a lot and we had always been able to work out our troubles. Then she began to hang around with some women on our block who had divorced their husbands. Somehow they persuaded her to drop me because they convinced her our marriage was keeping her from having fun."

What a tragedy! And yet how many people every day allow the bad influence of those around them to lead them astray—farther and farther from the way they originally had intended to go. Be careful whom you choose as friends, because what they say will help make your decisions. Paul wrote, "Do not be misled: 'Bad company corrupts good character' " (1 Corinthians 15:33 NIV).

A Blueprint for Failure

Do you remember the story of Lot? He was the nephew of Abraham, the father of faith. Lot certainly knew right from wrong—he understood the laws of God. But he chose to associate with bad company. The Bible says that Lot took his family, his flocks, and his herds, "and pitched his tent toward Sodom" (Genesis 13:12).

The people of Sodom and Gomorrah were wicked and depraved, and Lot knew this, yet he chose them to be his neighbors and in-laws. Only five chapters later we find that Lot's two daughters married men from that corrupt city. His wife came to love the home and possessions they had accumulated in Sodom, and apparently she also enjoyed the friendship of her depraved neighbors.

Then came the time when the cities of Sodom and Gomorrah became so evil in God's sight that they had to be destroyed. You will remember that there were not even 10 righteous people to be found in the entire metropolis. Because of Abraham's prayers and God's mercy, angels came to lead Lot and his family out of the city before judgment fell.

There was no time to move out all of Lot's possessions, herds, and flocks. His daughters' husbands refused to leave. Finally Lot, with his wife and two daughters, escaped with just the clothes they had on their backs. They were barely out of the city when fire and brimstone fell and completely destroyed the cities and all the surrounding area. Disobeying the clear instructions of God's angel messengers, Lot's wife looked back longingly at Sodom and was turned into a pillar of salt.

What a price Lot paid for his choice of evil companions! All his wealth was destroyed. His daughters' husbands were killed. And His wife perished also.

But that's not the end of the story. Just a few verses later the Bible gives the shameful account of how Lot's daughters each got him drunk and committed incest with him so that they could have children to carry on the family.

The Painful Penalty for Bad Relationships

Can you think of a more heartbreaking example of the devastating results of evil associations? Lot had been wealthy and prosperous, with a beautiful family. He was a close relative of Abraham, God's man of faith and yet Lot failed to manage his relationships properly. In just a few short years, everything in the world he held dear had been polluted and destroyed by the people he chose to associate with. His herds and possessions were destroyed. His daughters' families were wiped out. His own wife was a tragic victim.

In the end, Lot's own daughters—no doubt influenced by what they had learned in Sodom—duped him into committing incest with them. The children born as a result—Moab and

Ben-ammi—became the heads of entire tribes or nations. The Moabites and Ammonites were idolaters and followers of strange gods. Almost every time you read about them in the Old Testament they are warring against God's chosen people.

What a bitter irony that the descendants of Abraham's nephew, Lot, became some of the most persistent enemies of God!

Yet, it pays to be selective when choosing your personal friends. They are going to have a positive or negative influence on your life. The crowd you run with is going to determine to a great measure what your outcome in life is going to be. As Shakespeare said, "I am a part of everything I have seen and heard."

The Promise for Proper Associations

But as always, the Bible says it best: "Blessed is the man that walketh not in the counsel of the ungodly, nor standeth in the way of sinners, nor sitteth in the seat of the scornful" (Psalm 1:1).

And what is the reward of of a man who chooses good associates rather than bad ones? "He shall be like a tree planted by the rivers of water, that bringeth forth his fruit in his season; his leaf also shall not wither, and whatsoever he doeth shall prosper" (Psalm 1:3).

What a fantastic promise! First there is *security*. Like the tree planted by the river, your source of supply is never far away.

Second, there is *fruitfulness*. There is hardly anything more satisfying or fulfilling than to see your efforts produce good results.

Third, there is *protection*. How comforting to know that our lives will not dry up and burn out from the withering heart of oppression!

Fourth, there is *prosperity*. This is not just money or accumulated possessions. The promise specifically spells out that *everything* you touch will turn out right—that every endeavor will be successful.

So be careful who your friends are. Don't listen to the advice of the ungodly. Don't associate with sinners. Stay away from the company of the scornful. They can keep you from reaching your goals in life. They can keep you from prosperity.

The writer of Hebrews admonishes us to "be not slothful, but followers of them who through faith and patience inherit the promises" (Hebrews 6:12). So build positive relationships. Choose wholesome, successful associates. Manage your relationships, for this is the first natural law you must observe to achieve supernatural prosperity.

Chapter 3
HOW TO BE RICH IN MIND AND BODY

Shakespeare's poetic words, " 'Tis the mind that makes the body rich," underscore the great natural law for success and prosperity: apply your mind to the right concepts. *What* you think and *how* you think shapes your life and molds your future. As Cicero said, "The mind of each man is the man himself."

If you are not happy and successful, it is because your thoughts are wrong, for your life is a result of your thinking. Every day you are reaping the results of the thoughts you have sown. If you think right, you will live right. If you think wrong, you will live wrong. Mark Twain went so far as to say that the chief function of the body is to carry around the brain.

The human brain is one of the most powerful forces in all the universe. Consider, if you will, the knowledge contained in millions of books stored in thousands of libraries around the world. Listen to the intricate melodies and complex harmonies of the great musical works that have been composed over the centuries. Look at the fantastically beautiful works of art, the towering architectural marvels of modern civilization, the space-age technology that has produced almost unbelievable achievements in transportation and communication—all the complicated technology that has been devised to produce a more comfortable lifestyle for mankind. Realize that each one of these fantastic achievements once existed alone as a single idea in the mind of a man.

Manage Your Mind

Modern man uses only about one-tenth of his total potential in life. That is one of the most staggering facts we will ever face. Think of all the accomplishments, dreams, victories, and gifts that have never been realized throughout the lifetime of men on earth. Think of the 90 percent of you that now lies totally ignored and untapped. Think of all you could give yourself and your family if you used only 5 percent more of yourself than you are now using!

And how can you use more of yourself? By learning to manage your mind!

First of all, it is important that you *think*. Second, *what* you think is vital. Third, *how* you think determines whether you will be a failure or a success, a pauper or a prince of prosperity!

I am convinced that there are some people in the world who make a deliberate, all-out effort never to think about anything. They arrange their lives into a series of habits and routines that require the least amount of conscious effort. They choose entertainment and pastimes that deliberately do not challenge the intellect. They avoid discussions that require a considered opinion on their part. They seldom read anything more challenging than a cereal box. And they spend every spare waking minute sitting blank-faced in front of a televison set viewing unrealistic fables.

When these people *do* employ their minds, what do they think about? To talk with some men and women, you'd think the only things that ever occupied their minds were soap operas, situation comedies, and sports. What they think about is totally nonproductive.

Garbage In—Garbage Out

They remind me of the modern computer term—GIGO. It is a term used by computer technicians to explain that if bad information is programmed into the computer, bad results will come out. They call it Garbage In—Garbage Out!

The same rule applies to the marvelous computer of your mind. If you permit garbage thoughts to cloud up your mind, your life is going to be garbage.

What do you read when you pick up a newspaper? Do your eyes run to the editorial page? Do you search for the articles that will challenge your mind to make you a better person? Do you desire to learn something helpful?

Some people read only the society page, the sports page, or the comics. While there may be nothing wrong with these features, they are chaff compared to the wheat. Several years ago I read that an individual could actually get the equivalent of a college education by reading the editorial page of a good daily newspaper. We need to entertain our minds with things that matter.

The truth is that leaders are readers! If you want to be a leader and to succeed in helping others, then become a reader. It is a law that works. Feed your mind with good things.

You Are What You Read

I know some people who fill their minds with trash by reading only gossip columns, movie magazines, and the best-selling books, which are often filled with sordid and pornographic material.

Then there are people who short-circuit themselves with worry. They imagine every possible thing that could go wrong and every possible calamity that could befall them. Every time the phone rings they expect bad news, and every knock at the door makes them wonder what's gone wrong. Yet psychiatric examiners have found that 97 percent of the things people worry about never come to pass. Isn't that ironic?

Did you hear about the woman who had so many things to worry about she couldn't remember them all? Finally she made a list of them to carry around with her. Then she lost the list—and worried about that.

I like the comment of the old wash-woman who was asked how she stayed so happy all the time. She said, "When I work, I work hard. When I sit, I rest easy. When I worry, I go to sleep."

The Bible makes it clear that to be successful, we should feed our minds on good things. "Finally, brethren, whatsoever things are true, whatsoever things are honest, whatsoever things are just, whatsoever things are pure, whatsoever things are lovely, whatsoever things are of good report; if there be any virtue, and if there be any praise, think on these things" (Philippians 4:8).

Set Your Goals

Success begins with desire. A man must want to succeed and must apply his mind to setting goals he wishes to reach. It's important to set goals. If a person doesn't have goals, how will he know when he ever accomplishes anything worthwhile? How can he know what to pray for if he doesn't have goals? What would it take—financially, physically, and spiritually—for him to be what he would like to be? *He must decide that first,* being honest and realistic. Then he must be willing to set aside the time needed to reach his objectives. Finally, he must work out a plan to reach his goal.

Man is limited only by the obstacles he creates in his own mind. Educators have determined that there is almost nothing an individual cannot learn if he applies his mind to it. Most millionaires have paid a great price of courage, discipline, desire, and hard work, all focused on their goal of achievement. Frequently the millionaire has fewer natural talents than many people who slouch in front of a television set. But he steered and directed his every effort to get him nearer his goal. And when "breaks" and good fortune came along, he was ready to take full advantage of them.

A person with a job who never tries to improve his knowledge, ability, or skill does not deserve to be promoted or to make progress. One man was told, "You don't have ten years' experience. You have one year's experience ten times over, that's all!

Wise Ambition

John Dean, who was closely associated with the Nixon administration, wrote an interesting book entitled *Blind Ambition*. In the book he said, "If you want to be successful, volunteer for the jobs no one else wants. Even if you don't know how to do the work, you can soon learn. In so doing you make yourself so valuable your employer can't do without you. You rise in importance and are promoted. This increases your income."

We may not agree with all of Mr. Dean's politics or other activities, but in this case his advice is sound. You can put this to work at your own job. If you honestly believe that your own employer would never recognize your efforts and reward you for it, then by all means change jobs as soon as you can.

You can learn what you must know to achieve success in your chosen field. It doesn't matter if you have too little formal education. All professions and leading business positions require more home study than class instruction. One doctor told me that 90 percent of his education was derived by home study after he had completed his classes.

This country is full of libraries. It is full of opportunities. And it is ready to reward people who are willing to apply their minds and think the right things. The Bible says, "The plans of the diligent lead surely to advantage" (Proverbs 21:5).

To be truly successful and prosperous, you must learn the laws of prosperity. Have you ever asked someone who has a reputation for being a good money manager for suggestions or practical tips? Have you ever talked with your banker? You talk with your doctor when you need medical advice, so why not go to a professional when you need help with your money? I also suggest that you read some good money-management books and publications. Get Sylvia Porter's *Money Book*. It could save you $10,000 over a five-year period. Or read *Money Magazine, Changing Times,* or *Consumer's Digest.* Most people never study money—they just spend it. That is definitely *not* the path to prosperity.

Think Positive

Many psychologists, surgeons, and researchers are beginning to affirm that what we think about ourselves and how we go about it is the single most important factor in the quality of life.

Dr. Maxwell Maltz discovered the magic of self-image in his work as a plastic surgeon. He tells of thousands of cases in which he did remarkable plastic surgery only to find that the patient still felt he or she was unattractive or outright ugly. To make the surgery successful, he had to change their self-image—how they thought about themselves. Then in many cases he found that patients coming to him did not need any cosmetic surgery at all—just a change in their self-concept. They felt ugly because of the way they were thinking.

During each waking hour, our actions and statements reflect what we really feel about ourselves. As human beings, we have the power to change our thoughts and actions according to our beliefs. The power for positive change is a divine gift to man and man alone.

Your Mind Is a Computer

Dr. Maltz wrote a remarkable book titled *Psycho-Cybernetics*, based on his lifelong research. The book includes his extensive studies on the exciting relationship between the conscious and subconscious minds.

Dr. Maltz feels that the conscious mind is like a computer programmer feeding information into a computer. The information going in is strictly controlled by the programmer. He has the final say in what is right and wrong. The computer, on the other hand, can act only on the information it is given, plus the information in the memory bank.

Our conscious mind determines *what* we will think about certain issues. We are consciously capable of judging on moral questions and deciding whether a course of action is right or wrong. Then, like the computer programmer, we send our decisions to our subconscious mind through our thoughts, actions, and words. Our subconscious mind can only take what information is fed in—good or bad—and act on it. Like the computer, our subconscious minds obey every command and feed the appropriate and genius is self-bestowed."

There is one other important difference between the conscious and the subconscious. Our conscious mind has the use of all the external senses—vision, touch, hearing, taste, and smell—to tell what is real and what is imaginary. The subconscious mind takes all the information sent to it from the conscious level as if it were all real. It has no senses that touch reality, so it cannot tell the real from the imaginary.

The Way You Want to Be

What does all this mean? The benefit to you as a human being is that you can use the subconscious to improve your conscious activities. By mentally seeing yourself doing what you want to be able to do, you put a picture in your subconscious mind that the subconscious takes as real. So the subconscious mind immediately begins acting as if that were the case.

Millions of people all over the world become self-programmed to believe that they *cannot!* These "cannot" people defeat themselves at every turn, before they ever reach a problem. Their subconscious mind is programmed negatively, for it has been told by the *conscious* mind that the person is incapable of any significant accomplishment. The subconscious takes that message as fact!

You Can!

The trick to living life to the fullest is to become a *can do* person. By programming the subconscious mind with positive, affirmative beliefs, the subconscious immediately approaches every challenge as though you were a winner.

Some of the world's greatest athletes take advantage of this and practice subconsciously when they are unable to work out and practice physically. They program imaginary practice sessions. The subconscious mind reacts as if the athlete had been out in the field actually practicing. By pretending mentally to be hitting a golf ball, golf pros can actually improve their swing without physically hitting the ball.

Dr. Maltz found that positive substitution was one of the most effective methods of changing the self-image. This calls for the individual to substitute thoughts of what he would like to be for those negative thoughts he had been having.

Earl Nightingale, a leading spokesman for the self-improvement movement, often says, "We become what we think about the most." If we constantly think negative, limiting, defeated thoughts, that's exactly what we become. On the other hand, if we think positive, creative, winning thoughts, we find ourselves being molded into our powerful new self-image.

Go Where You Want to Go

The person who is willing to change for the better and grow in his self-image can move from where he is to anywhere he wants to go. A man named Walter Russell believed this so strongly that he declared, "Mediocrity is self-inflicted, and genius is self-bestowed."

The Bible says simply, "As a man thinketh in his heart, so is he" (Proverbs 23:7). How are you thinking? Are you crying with the defeated, "Woe is me, I am undone," or are you saying with the Apostle Paul, "I can do all things through Christ, who strengthens me?"

Og Mandino, who wrote *The Greatest Salesman in the World,* advised that we should affirm, "I am God's greatest creation. He gave me abilities and powers superior to any other creature on the face of the earth. There is no limit to what I can accomplish."

He further advises that we should remember to say, "I am unique! There is no other person on the face of the earth who is exactly like me. No one who has ever lived since time began has had exactly the same talents, abilities, and skills that I possess. No one who shall live after me will be able to duplicate the contribution I can make."

The person who thinks like this will be successful in whatever he sets out to do.

Use Your Mind to Get Ahead

This brings us to a restatement of the second basic natural law for success and prosperity: *Apply your mind to the right concepts.* This is expressed beautifully in Psalm 1:2: "His delight is in the law of the Lord, and in His law he doth meditate day and night." And what is the law of the Lord? Is it a series of "Thou shall nots?" No, indeed! The law of the Lord is fulfilled in the Great Commandment of Jesus: "Love God with all your heart, soul, strength, and mind, and love your neighbor as yourself" (Luke 10:27).

If you want to attain supernatural prosperity, it's time for you to check up on yourself. First of all, *are you thinking?* Are you consciously using your mind to help you reach your goal in life?

Second, *what are you thinking about?* Are you flooding your mind with garbage, or are you filling it with useful, important information that can help you solve the challenges of daily living?

Finally, *how are you thinking?* Are you thinking positively, hopefully, in faith? Or do you short-circuit any changes you have for success by programming your mental computer with negativism and a failure image?

What you think, you are. So observe the advice of Napoleon Hill—"Think and grow rich!"

Chapter 4
HOW TO GET MORE LIFE OUT OF YOUR TIME

Time is life!

The basic resource which each person starts out with is the minutes, hours, days, and years that will make up his lifetime. Whatever your position in life, you have the same amount of this precious commodity as everyone else alive. Whether your name is Rockefeller, Ford, Edison, Smith, Jones, or Lundstrom, you have exactly 24 hours in every day.

Most of us fail to realize—or we forget—that we have less than 100,000 waking hours in a lifetime and less than 10,000 working days. Life is terribly short. If you begin your career at the age of 21 and retire at age 65, you have only 528 months to fulfill your mission in life.

I didn't realize until a short time ago that an average person spends 24 years of his lifetime in bed. This is easy to figure out—simply divide a 24-hour day into three periods. Allow 8 hours for work, 8 hours for sleep, and 8 hours for free time. You will discover that one-third of a man's lifespan of 72 years—or 24 years—is spent in bed.

Let's break it down a little more. You and I are speeding toward death at the rate of 60 minutes per hour. Life is so short that if you're 18 years old and live to be 70, you have only 2800 weeks left to live. If you are 30 and reach 70, you have 2000 weeks; if you are 40, you have only 1500 weeks until age 70; if you are 50, you have only 1000 weeks. And if you are 60, you have only 500 weeks until you are boxed and buried.

Benjamin Franklin said, "Dost thou love life? Then do not squander time, for that is the stuff life is made of." Because time is irreversible and irreplaceable, wasting time is literally wasting your life.

Always Enough Time

If you're like most people I know, your most common complaint is that you're too busy to get everything done. There just don't seem to be enough hours in the day or enough days in the week to accomplish all the tasks and projects you'd like to get done.

Would it surprise you to know that there is no such thing as lack of time? We all have plenty of time to do everything we really want to do. There are plenty of people who are even busier than you are who manage to get more done than you do. Is it because they are smarter or more skilled? Absolutely not! They simply have learned to use their time to better advantage. In fact, organizations that depend on volunteer help have learned that they get much greater results by asking the help of busy people rather than those who appear to have all the time in the world. *Busy people get things done!*

There simply isn't anything more important than your time. We all must live on 168 hours a week. If you aren't satisfied with how much you're getting done in life, it's time to do something about it. If you constantly feel harried, frustrated, and rushed, it's a pretty safe bet that you need to learn how to manage your time better. How do you do it? It's really fairly simple.

Plan Your Work and Work Your Plan

Control of your time starts with planning. Planning is bringing the future into the present so you can do something about it now. What do you have to do today? To increase the likelihood of getting everything accomplished, you have to know exactly what tasks you must work on—and when you will do them. No matter how busy you are, you must always take time to plan. In fact, the less time you feel you have to spare, the more important it is to plan your time carefully. Robert Schuller, whose Hour of Power television show is seen across the country, says, "Failing to plan is planning to fail!"

How do you go about planning your time? Let me show you by example.

Charlie Schwab was a pretty competent executive. A former president of Bethlehem Steel, he was one of the few men ever to be paid a million dollars a year. His company didn't pay him that kind of money just because he looked good sitting in a swivel chair behind a big desk. At times, however, Schwab wasn't as satisfied with his performance as other people were. He felt he wasn't getting enough done. Details and minor matters were crowding the time that he urgently needed for more important problems.

Mr. Schwab asked Ivy Lee, a forerunner of the modern business consultant, what to do about it. Lee handed Schwab a blank sheet of paper.

"Write down the six most important things you have to do tomorrow," he said. "Tomorrow morning start on Item 1 and work on it till it's finished. Then go to the next item."

The steel executive tried the idea and recommended it to his associates. It worked so well that he reportedly sent Lee a check for $25,000 in appreciation.

Make a Daily List

That simple plan will work for you! Each day

make a list of the items you have to do. You'll be amazed at how much more you'll accomplish by simply having a visual reminder of what must be done!

Write all your "to do" items on a single list rather than jotting them down on various scraps of paper. That way your list is always available as a reference to see what you should work on next.

But it is not enough to simply list the things you have to do! The next step is to arrange your list in order of priority, doing the most important task first, then going to the second most important task, and so on. Some people spend all their time working on trivial tasks—things that aren't really very important. Too often they come to the end of the day with all the low-priority jobs finished, and none of the really important tasks even begun.

Making the right choices about how you use your time is more important than being efficient in doing whatever job happens to be around. Efficiency is fine in its place, but in my opinion *effectiveness* is a much more important goal. That's why it is so crucial that each day you plan your work by listing what you have to do and arranging the tasks in the priority you will do them.

The 80/20 Rule

A time-planning expert has discovered what he calls the 80/20 Rule. He says that in any list of things to do, you will find that 80 percent of the value you receive from those tasks comes from doing only 20 percent of the items, while the remaining 20 percent of the value comes from the other 80 percent.

In other words, in a list of 10 items, two of them will yield 80 percent of the value of all the jobs you will do that day. To be successful in the use of your time, find these two items and get them done first. If necessary, leave most of the other eight undone, because the value from them is significantly less than from those two high-value items you work on first.

Know Your Use of Time

Without some sort of time-planning system it's almost impossible to know how you spend your time. Most of us don't use our time the way we think we do. If you really checked up on the things you did hour-by-hour in a typical week, I think you would be amazed at the time you've spent on relatively unimportant matters. You would be shocked by the small amount of time you devoted to the major problems of your job or your household.

This happens because humans are made that way. The man who does not plan his time—budgeting so much for this and so much for that—exposes himself to certain strong natural influences. One of these is what we call Parkinson's First Law: "Work expands so as to fill the time available for its completion."

When people feel there's no rush to get something done, it usually takes three or four times as long as if they had set a deadline for that task. Almost always they spend more time on the job than it's actually worth.

I heard about a man who decided he was going to take Wednesday afternoons off during the summer to play golf. Almost without exception he arrived at the golf course full of pep, raring to go, claiming that he had accomplished as much on Wednesday morning as he usually did in a full day! And it was probably true. Working with the knowledge that he had only a half-day at his disposal, he really made the minutes count. That's what is really important. Life is not measured by the years of time we live, but by what we have accomplished during those years.

Given two people of equal ability, the one who plans his time more effectively will far outperform the other. He will make time for the creative thinking and problem-solving which are vital to his job. The other person will put them off until he finds time—until the opportunities are lost and his problems become so critical that they demand immediate belated attention.

Peter Drucker, who wrote the book *The Effective Executive*, said that nothing distinguishes successful businessmen as much as their tender loving care of time.

150 or 5?

Recently I came across one of the most amazing stories of what can be accomplished through successful time management. At the beginning of World War Two, America began building Liberty ships for the Navy to use in the war effort. It took 150 days to build one ship.

Because our need for ships was so desperate, the word went out that the time had to be cut down drastically. The builders analyzed all procedures involved in constructing a ship and reorganized the plant with speed in mind. The time was cut down to 72 days.

But the planners didn't stop there. They kept working, coming up with new ideas and new time-saving proposals. Soon the time was down to 46 days—then to 29 days. After more changes and more ideas for proper use of time, a ship was built in 10 days. Finally, toward the end of the war, the Robert E. Peary was completed in an incredible 4 days, 15½ hours!

Don't Waste Time

Are you a person who likes to kill time? The best way to do it is to work it to death! Lost time means lost opportunity, and lost opportunity means lost money.

What do you do with the time you spend waiting? Almost everybody has to wait for people to show up for appointments, for buses, for planes, for trains to cross road intersections, or for your family to get ready to go to church or to a meeting. Do you put your waiting time to good use, or do you waste it by pacing up and down or sitting idly by, perhaps getting more irritable as the minutes pass?

Waiting time is perfect for reading, thinking through problems, or planning.

I know people who carry small books or magazines like *Reader's Digest* in their car. Any time they have to wait—for a long traffic light or for a train to pass—they grab their book and read a page or two.

If you have an especially tricky problem, use your waiting time to think it through. First, try outlining the problem step-by-step. Then pick out an aspect that might be thoroughly explored in that five-minute period of time.

Or carry a pad and pencil and do your planning for the rest of the day, or for tomorrow.

You may discover that your waiting time which had once been totally wasted can now become one of the more productive parts of your entire day.

Many people even try to make their sleep work for them. They pose a question to their subconscious minds just before they fall asleep. They select a problem that requires hours of thought. They spend no time thinking about it consciously, but they allow the subconscious to focus on it while they are asleep, and they expect a meaningful answer when they awaken.

Spare Time—Success or Failure?

The one area where most people succeed or fail is that of spare time. Isn't it strange that if given a chance to do anything in the world they want to do, some people do nothing?

Charles Lamb was a clerk in his daily work, but his books—written in his spare time—are his true monuments. Samuel Morse was an artist, but he invented the telegraph in his spare time. A teacher in an obscure college used to tinker with an odd-looking contraption in his spare time. He built a monument to his name—the Bell Telephone.

Richard Baxter once said, "Spend your time in nothing that you know must be repented of, in nothing on which you might not pray for the blessings of God." That's pretty good advice, don't you think?

The Bible says, "Teach us to number our days, that we may present to Thee a heart of wisdom" (Psalm 90:12).

Perhaps one of the best planning tools to help you use your time wisely is to know what your goals are. A written lifetime goal statement will give direction to your life. Writing out your goals requires you to be specific. Then, as you look at what you've written, it's easy to determine if the way you are now spending your time is helping you reach the goals you have set. As the country philosopher said, "The man who doesn't know where he's going will never know when he gets there!"

Concentrate on Today

A word of caution about time—the most important day in your whole life is the one you're living right now. Don't allow yourself to be overly concerned about yesterday, last week, or last month. Nor should you focus your attention so much on tomorrow and the future that today is used up in dreaming.

There are two days in every week you should never worry about. One is yesterday, with its mistakes, faults, blunders, aches, and pains. Yesterday has passed forever beyond your control. All the money in the world cannot bring it back. You cannot undo a single act or erase a single word. Yesterday is gone forever, beyond recall.

The other day you should not worry about is tomorrow, with its possible adversities, its burdens, its large promise, and perhaps its poor performance. Tomorrow is also beyond your control. Until tomorrow's sun rises, you have no stake in it because it is yet unborn.

This leaves only today for you to concentrate on. Anybody can fight the battles of just one day. It is only when we add the burdens of those two awful eternities, yesterday and tomorrow, that we break down. It is not the experience of today that drives men mad, but the remorse of what happened yesterday, or the dread of what tomorrow might bring.

So continually ask yourself, "What is the best use of my time *right now?*"

Make Your Time Count

Force yourself to action by making a commitment. *Set a deadline, and make yourself keep it.* This technique is especially valuable to help you take care of those sometimes-unpleasant tasks that you have a tendency to put off forever.

Another way to avoid getting bogged down and staying involved in tasks unnecessarily is to always set a next step. Frequently a project will bog down for lack of knowing what to do next. When you are working your way through a particular assignment, make a clear plan for what the next step is to be. Then set a time to check whether you have completed that step.

Perhaps the one thing which all successful people seem to have in common is a concern for the proper use of time. If you would be successful and supernaturally prosperous, you must make your time count.

Chapter 5
HOW TO KEEP YOUR MONEY FROM COSTING TOO MUCH

The fourth natural law for success and prosperity is to manage your money.

"You might say, "That should be easy for me, because I don't have any."

But you do! A fortune is going to pass through your hands during your lifetime. To be able to manage your money, you must be able to view your life's earnings at one time. If you earn $1000 a month and are now 20, you will handle almost one-half million dollars before retirement—if you never get a raise in pay. Do a little quick checking right now! Multiply your average monthly income times the number of months since you first started working. How much does it come to?

Perhaps a better question is, how much of the money you have earned do you still have? If you are wise, you will plan your earnings in such a way as to have accumulated a significant amount by the end of your working life.

Since most of us are not born into great wealth

and do not have a fortune handed to us to start out on, it is necessary for us to find a way to earn money. We are indeed fortunate to live in the greatest country in the world—America, the land of opportunity. Despite all its problems, faults, and injustices (pointed out so quickly by its critics), the United States still affords greater opportunities to those who want to achieve something than any other country in the world.

Once you have found your opportunity, give it all you've got. The Bible says, "Whatsoever thy hand findeth to do, do it with thy might" (Ecclesiastes 9:10).

Expand Your Earning Power

I have found that the majority of Americans are content to hold down a job, then pick up a check. Very few are willing to apply themselves to learning, so that they can truly increase their income. If you want to make a good living, you'd better learn how to use your head. Read new books in areas of interest. Apply for a course that teaches a trade you'd like to learn on the side. Keep learning, keep studying, keep at it!

If you settle down to a regular 40-hour week doing the same thing day after day, chances are that a crisis will arise and you will be swept away. If you can learn a second or even a third trade, it will help you keep your options open. Someone has said, "A mouse with only one hole is soon caught." If you are one of the millions of Americans with only one hole, don't be surprised if you get caught in a financial bind.

Another tip you might keep in mind is to utilize the full manpower of your household. I've known parents who have encouraged their children to have paper routes so they could earn their own money for their clothing. There's a lot of money to be made even by the least active members of the household: baby-sitting, working on telephone surveys, even raking leaves—there's a host of odd jobs that can help bring extra money into your home.

If the members of your household have good health, there's a lot of money that can be earned. If a man or woman is willing to work, there is always someone willing to pay an honest wage. If finances are pinched in your home, review your troops. There might be quite a number that need to get into the budget battle.

Waste Not, Want Not

There are thousands of Americans who don't know about managing their money. They waste as much or more of their income than they use profitably. The result is absolute tragedy.

Jesus condemned waste and encouraged thrifty use of resources. When he fed the multitude of 5000 people with a boy's lunch, He instructed His disciples afterwards, "Gather up the fragments that remain, that nothing be lost" (John 6:12).

Failure to use money wisely causes more heartache and trouble than you can imagine. I am told that 65 percent of Americans are in financial difficulty—that is, they spend at least 100 percent of their income each year. At least 5 percent of them owe between 75 and 100 percent of their yearly income. Americans owe between 10 and 15 billion dollars of overdue bills. One out of every four dollars spent in this country goes for debts!

What happens when a family has more debts than it can pay? Big trouble. One of the main reasons for men skipping home is money. A sociological research project in Chicago discovered that more than 40 percent of the desertion cases there were rooted in financial tension between husband and wife, while 45 percent of the reported cases of cruelty were the result of financial tension.

More than half of the families who seek counseling have money problems. An astounding *90 percent* of all divorces involved money conflicts—and in more than half of these, money was the major cause of the divorce.

Why are there so many money problems in our country today? Some people say it is partly because Americans have become so "thing"-oriented—cars, furniture, clothing, sporting goods, color TV's, stereos, albums—the list is endless. Our happiness and well-being seem to hinge directly around the acquisition of things.

Watch Your Credit

Someone else has suggested that our money problems are to a large degree due to too much easy credit. We have come to live in a credit-card society.

I heard about one wife who told her husband, "The dollar keeps losing value—we're lucky we use credit cards!"

Another lady out on a shopping spree said to a friend, "I just love credit cards—they go so much farther than money."

Credit cards are convenient, but terribly dangerous because they encourage compulsive buying. They fuel our temptation to buy things we don't need and haven't yet earned. Almost all of today's credit comes with extremely costly charges built in. When fully analyzed, you'll usually discover that credit card charges range from 12 to 20 percent per year.

Another danger is that credit cards often encourage you to spend more than you should for a particular item, merely because of the convenience. One expert says that if you use service station credit cards, you may be spending up to 32 percent more for automobile servicing than if you did it yourself and paid cash.

The problem is that you don't think in terms of spending money when you use your credit card. Simply signing your name to a little slip with the knowledge that the bill will come later (and be paid over a period of time) seems to make it all right to keep buying and buying. So your debt gets bigger and bigger.

Go over a list of your recent credit purchases. Which of the items you charged did you need and which could you have done without?

If you are honest with yourself, you may discover that you probably could have done without the majority of the items you bought on credit. Another good question to ask yourself: If you had not been carrying the credit card and had to either pay cash or write a check for that item, would you have bought it?

One financial expert says that credit cards should not be used for general purchasing or money management. A good rule of thumb is that you should be able to reduce your outstanding credit card balance in no more than 60 days without disturbing your budget. If you find yourself consistently making the minimum payment required on a credit-card account, that should signal you that you are not using your credit cards well.

Be Interested in Interest

Of course, there are other kinds of credit besides charge cards. There is the installment account—or the easy-payment plan—which enables you to make a sizable purchase by dividing the purchase price into 12, 18, or 24 monthly payments. Interest is added for this privilege. And it is expensive. I'm told that the average new-car loan in 1977 was for 44 months! With interest, these buyers will pay for their cars almost twice!

Then there is "revolving credit," in which you pay on your total debt and are still allowed to add to that debt up to a set amount. Many department stores provide this kind of credit.

Anytime you borrow money you don't have, you must pay rent on that money. That rent is called interest. If you borrow against the cash value of a life-insurance policy, you will pay 6 or 7 percent. If you borrow at the bank, the rate will range from 9 to 12.5 percent. A finance company will charge from 18 to 25 percent. A credit union normally charges from 10 to 12 percent, and retail installment credit is even higher. When you purchase something for which that kind of interest will be charged, ask yourself if its total purchase price is really worth that much more money.

I realize that we live in a credit society, and that it is nearly impossible to exist without some credit accounts. Few families can purchase everything they need on a cash-only basis. At times credit buying can be a good thing, but it must be recognized as *a power which needs control.* Financial consultants suggest that 20 to 25 percent of one's income is the maximum that should be committed to installment debt.

Good stewardship in the Christian life demands that a man take good care of his financial affairs because he has been commissioned by Christ to manage those affairs for the Lord. This requires planning.

Everyone agrees that money is important. But planning *how to use money* may be more important than the money itself. Materials are important to the building of a house, but it is obvious that the blueprint by which all that material is to be brought together into a fine home is more important than the building materials. Your *time and energy* represent the raw material which go into your particular work or job. However, *control* of your time and energy is far more important than either of these two items alone.

Manage Your Financial Resources

When it comes to money, good planning means establishing a budget. Many people cringe when they hear that word. They look upon a budget as a nuisance or a necessary evil. Actually, it can be one of the best friends you will ever have. A good budget is an invaluable and necessary aid to managing your money efficiently.

In life, we find that when we establish boundaries for ourselves we're much more comfortable. This is true with our children. The child who is insecure and a discipline problem is a child who has never had adequate boundaries. To be totally disciplined, you need to govern all areas of your life—not only your Bible reading, your prayer life, and your church life, but also your financial affairs. The startling fact is that if you're not operating on a budget, you are wasting between $50 and $175 a month.

Two of the best books I have read on this subject are George Bowman's *How to Succeed with Your Money* and Malcolm McGregor's *Your Money Matters.* I have given away thousands of these fine books to my friends all over the country. In both books, the authors talk about a budget system called the 10-70-20 plan. I think it is the most sound and simple budget plan I've ever heard about, and I recommend it to you.

In its most simple form, the 10-70-20 plan is this: After paying your tithes and standard taxes, save 10 percent of the balance, live on 70 percent, and use 20 percent to pay debts.

Pay Yourself First

Let's look at those categories a little closer. First of all, the budget says that you should pay yourself before you pay your debts. I know it may not sound right at first, but experience shows that the man who *saves* before he *spends* enjoys financial health.

So after you have looked after your obligation to God and paid your taxes, set aside 10 percent of the remaining amount for savings and investments. You see, you don't get rich on the money you work for. It's the money that *works for you* that makes the difference.

If you were given a $1000 bill, the chances are that your reaction would be—"What can I buy with this money?" If the same amount were given to a serious financial planner, his reaction would be, "What can I *earn* with this money?" *That is the difference between financial failure and financial success.* It is far more important to *save money* than it is to *purchase things*.

Let's assume that you are 35 and earn a net income of $600 (after taxes and tithe). A 10-percent savings would be $60.00 per month. If you earned 7 percent profit (compounded each year), your savings at age 65 would be over $70,500. You would have deposited only $21,600 and gained a profit of $48,900. That is nearly seven years' income earned for you by the simple act of saving only two dollars a day!

If you accept the fact that you must get along without that 10 percent of your income, it will never be a burden to you. It is actually a small amount to buy financial health and peace of mind for you and your family. Doesn't it make sense that if you keep 10 percent of all you earn, you will always have money? Every person I know who has tried this for any length of time claims that the investment of his net income did not interfere with his present scale of living. And in the final analysis, you are worth what you saved, no matter how much you made.

Save for the Right Reasons

When we talk about savings, we need to be careful that we are not involved in saving strictly for the sake of saving, because that can lead to real problems. God warns His people to beware lest their accumulated wealth cause "thine heart to be lifted up, and then forget the Lord thy God"

(Deuteronomy 8:14; cp. 8:11-13). I think this is one of the biggest problems in the area of savings. "They that will be rich fall into temptation and a snare, and into many foolish and hurtful lusts, which drown men in destruction and perdition" (1 Timothy 6:9). So save with a purpose—to be able to give to God's work when special needs arise.

Great numbers of Americans live from paycheck to paycheck without saving a dime. In fact, salesmen will tell you that many people never ask the list price of merchandise. They'll usually say, "How much will it cost me a month?"

I've found that people who have money are very reluctant to spend it. Financially secure couples make it a regular practice to set aside savings. The savings need not always be in a bank account, but they need to be regularly invested in such a way that the money will return itself with interest within a few years.

Know Where Your Money Goes

When you talk about savings, many people will reply by saying, "I don't earn enough to save any money at all." But if you'll search carefully you'll find that this is not true. Millions of people all over the world could live on less than half of what the average American spends, and they'd have more than enough to spare.

Examine your spending. If you're using large amounts of money on perishable items like clothing, rent, amusements, liquor, tobacco, sporting goods, automobiles, and furniture, then you'd better rearrange your buying habits. Spend money on good solid merchandise. Make your spending count. Most immigrants who come to America and land a good job end up saving great amounts of money. One reason is that they do not allow themselves to get caught up with the many luxuries which most Americans call necessities.

One big obstacle to saving (apart from never starting a plan in the first place) is the temptation to stop saving and start spending. You are saving to *have money.* You cannot succeed with a plan to have money if you continually dip into your accumulated funds to pay for perishable things.

Another major obstacle to success with money is a common misunderstanding of the word "savings." Because of the influence of modern advertising, the word "savings" has come to mean "spending" in our society. Look at a newspaper ad or watch a commercial. How many of them say, "You save 15 percent," or "You save $7.00"? Many people are fooled into thinking they are saving money when they are in fact spending it. *You do not save money by spending it!*

But perhaps the greatest obstacle to success with money is delaying the start of a savings program. Putting it off causes more people to fail than all the other reasons put together. The way to overcome this is to pay yourself first! After you have paid your tithes and the standard taxes that are withheld from your check, then take 10 percent off the top.

Live on Your Income

The next section of the 10-70-20 budget plan is the money you use to live on. The easiest way to control your spending is to allot a certain percentage of your income to live on, and never go over that percentage. Be determined never to let your living costs rise higher than 7/10 of your *net* income. Living on 70 percent of your income seems to introduce an attitude of control over spending that produces more value for less money. You stop *spending* and start *shopping*, which means that you put more thought into how you spend your dollars.

The 70 percent you spend for living costs must cover your mortgage, rent, utilities, insurance, furniture, food, automobile, cleaning, medical attention, recreation, and entertainment.

You must plan your spending budget to fit

your individual requirements. The important thing to remember is to never allow your total living costs to exceed 70 percent of your net income.

To be a financial success, you must think things over all the time. First, you must ask yourself, "Do I really need what I'm planning to buy?" Then ask, "Is this proposition and the one who proposes it capable of filling my need?" Third, "What is it going to cost, and can I afford it?" Then make your decision based on the answers to your questions. Making purchases is important business.

I've heard of people who got bored and decided to take an evening out to go shopping— just for fun. "We don't have anything else to do, so let's go shopping," they say. And they spend money they don't have for frivolities they don't need. That is the height of stupidity!

Here's a rule that will save you hundreds, even thousands, of dollars. The rule is this: When a salesperson is all done making his pitch, say, "Thank you, we will let you know within a day or so what our decision is." The whole point is that you need to make your purchasing decisions *away from the pressure of the sales pitch.*

Ask Before You Buy

Anytime you're going to spend more than $50

on anything, ask these 10 questions: 1) "Do I really need this? 2) Is the price reasonable? 3) Is this the best time of the year to buy it? 4) If it is a bargain price, is it a current model? 5) If it is on sale, is it a true sale price? 6) Can I substitute something else for this? 7) Does this product have any major disadvantages? 8) Though excessive in price, will this satisfy an inner need? 9) Have I checked and researched the item? 10) Will the seller guarantee or stand behind the product?"

Take the time to ask these questions and think about your purchase, and you will be protected from impulse buying that causes big trouble for so many people. Checking out the quality of items before you buy them helps insure getting full value for your money. There are good magazines such as *Changing Times* and *Consumer Reports* which go to great lengths to evaluate various products. You can learn exactly what the features are, what the disadvantages are, and how the product performs under thorough testing.

One other tip is not to spend your money on cheap merchandise! One reason why poor people stay poor is that they have never learned how to spend their money wisely. My father used to drill me with the importance of buying good-quality merchandise. As a boy, I often owned only one pair of shoes, but I'll tell you, the shoes my father purchased for me were good ones! He didn't want me ruining my feet on clod-hoppers.

If you stand in a modern shopping center, you'll see people spending their money on junk. They'll buy a junk stereo for the same amount of money they could have purchased a high-quality used stereo. They'll buy plastic purses that tear apart in a few months. They'll buy women's shoes made of cardboard with heels that fall off. They'll buy cheap clothing that looks old after a few washings.

I would rather purchase something used of good quality than something new that was made cheaply. I'm not knocking the purchase of new merchandise as long as you can afford it and it's of good quality. But if you're a little pinched for money and you want to enjoy the best, be humble enough to search for bargains.

The Art of Grocery Shopping

Buying food is an important expenditure in your family budget. Here are some basic rules you can apply which will help you get the most value for your dollar. 1) Never go to the store hungry. 2) Shop no more often than once a week. 3) When you shop, use a list. Experts say that you should have a complete list of items you need from the store and should stick as closely to it as possible. This will enable you to go through the store without being enticed to pick up goodies you really didn't intend to buy and don't really need. Many women say that planning their meals for one or two weeks at a time dictates the shopping list for them.

Another tip is to take advantage of coupon offers. Don't let the coupons dictate what you will buy; instead, *first* decide what you are going to purchase and *then* see what coupons you have. Use those cents-off coupons when you make purchases.

One family discovered that on a $45.00 grocery bill they were able to use $4.00 worth of coupons—a 9 percent saving!

Another tip is to shop alone, since if you take somebody with you it will probably cost you more. Children influence the purchasing habits of their parents. And husbands are notorious for adding extra little goodies to the shopping cart.

When you're shopping, check the lower shelves—sometimes the same items can be bought at a cheaper price with very little sacrifice in quality. Almost all major food chains have their own house brands. Usually these are quality products, and you can save up to 15 percent just by buying them instead of name brands.

It's also important to understand unit pricing

on grocery items. This enables you to compare the price per ounce. One expert suggests that when buying vegetables, look for a target price of 1¼$^{¢}$ per ounce. On other items go for a target price per serving—perhaps 5$^{¢}$ per serving on fresh fruits and vegetables. This may mean that you have to buy smaller apples—but you will probably find that you're just as satisfied with a small piece of fruit as with a big one, and it has less calories besides.

Avoid junk foods. Often, the more food is processed, the more it costs and the less food value it has. Also, go easy on prepared foods or convenience foods. Most of them cost more than the same items prepared at home, and they're usually inferior in quality as well.

Look for Better Deals

Do comparison shopping. Shop for the specials offered by different stores. Don't overlook independent supermarkets—sometimes their specials and overall prices are lower than those of the big chain markets. When you find super bargain prices on some item, buy it in large quantities and freeze your supply. You will get better prices and you will get the items you really want if you simply shop the specials at your local stores.

When you find a real bargain on frying chickens, hamburger, roast beef, or whatever, don't buy just enough for one or two meals—stock your freezer. If you fill your freezer with vegetables and fruits bought inexpensively at peak-of-the-season prices, this can have a tremendous savings effect on your overall food bill. It's also a good idea to buy day-old breads and other bakery goods that keep in the freezer. By doing this you can stockpile inventories of nonperishable goods to be used throughout the year.

Simply following these and other common-sense suggestions may make it possible for you to cut your spending on food and grocery items by hundreds of dollars over a year's time. And because your meals will be better planned, you'll probably eat even better than you did before.

Buy Term Life Insurance

Here are a few helpful tips about life insurance. First of all, there is no such thing as life insurance; no contract can replace a human life. What you buy is *income* insurance—a plan to replace part of the income you would have earned had you lived. You can insure your income at a very low premium by purchasing *decreasing term* insurance. This is the best method to insure your income.

However, most insurance agents will not suggest that you buy term insurance. Instead, they will recommend another kind of policy—whole life, also known as straight life or ordinary life. "This policy gives you full coverage," the salesman tells you, "plus it accumulates a cash balance. It's really like a savings account for you!"

More often than not, the consumer ends up buying a whole-life policy, believing that it is a better deal for him because he is also building up a savings account. Unfortunately, there are some basic flaws in this course of action.

First of all, whole-life insurance is much more expensive than term insurance—usually four to five times more expensive. The average working man cannot afford as much whole-life insurance coverage as his family really needs. So he ends up buying much less coverage. Should the bread earner die, his family really doesn't have as much income protection as they will have to have. For a much lower monthly premium they could have bought adequate *term* insurance coverage.

There is another danger. Because the average insurance buyer feels he can hardly afford the high monthly premiums, the average duration of a whole-life policy is only seven years. Then the buyer gives up and lets the policy lapse, either to leave his family completely unprotected or, hopefully, to buy the increased protection his family really needs through term insurance.

The Great American Rip-off

But the real scandal comes in the "savings" section of the life-insurance program. Suppose you went to a bank or savings company to open a new account and asked someone to explain the benefits to you.

"Oh, it's quite simple," the officer replies. "You deposit a certain amount each month into this account. For the first year or two your savings will not accumulate—we'll keep what you deposit to cover some of our handling costs. But after that, every month your account will increase. Why, we'll even pay you 2½-3¼ percent interest on that money. In only 10 or 15 years you'll have a tidy little sum put back.

"And here's another benefit—if you need to take some of your money out of this savings account, we'll only charge you 5 or 6 percent interest on it.

"One last thing—you understand that if you die while you're doing business with our company, we'll keep your savings acount!"

If you heard this explanation from a bank or savings company, you would run—not walk—to get away from those crazy people. "How dumb do they think I am?" you'd say.

Yet that's exactly what millions of people are doing every day with life-insurance companies. Cash value in a whole-life-insurance policy does not begin accumulating until the second or third year. Then that money earns only 2½-3¼ percent interest. If you take the accumulated cash value out of your policy, you must either give up your life-insurance protection or pay interest on the money. Should you die during the insured term of your policy, your beneficiary would be paid the face value of the policy. But your so-called savings—the cash value of the policy—would be kept by the life-insurance company.

What it boils down to is this: Buy your life insurance from an insurance company. Do your savings with a bank or savings-and-loan firm.

Remember this: All insurance is "term" insurance. You simply pay much more for it when it is called by another name.

Debt Is the Worst Poverty

The third section of your budget is designed to help you get out of debt. Getting rid of back bills has always been a major financial problem for most people. Excessive debt usually indicates a personality weakness to overspend. If that is the case, never buy anything on credit again. Return or destroy all your charge plates and credit cards and go on a strictly-cash basis. Here's how

George Bowman suggests that you pay your back debts without pain.

First, make a list of all your creditors, including their full names, addresses, and phone numbers.

Second, work out exactly what you owe each of them.

Third, calculate what 20 percent of your net income is (after tithes and taxes).

Fourth, determine the total amount of money you owe by adding the figures after your creditors' names.

Fifth, work out the percentage of total debt that you owe each creditor. For example, if your total debts are $5000 and you owe the bank $1000, that's 20 percent of the total.

Sixth, take those percentage figures and put them beside the amounts you owe your creditors.

Seventh, apply the percentage figures to the amount of money you have allowed for paying debts—or 20 percent of your net income. This will tell you how much to allot to each creditor.

In his book, George Bowman tells of a man he counseled who followed his advice. The man went to see each of his creditors to tell them of his new plan and the revised amount of the payment they could expect from him. He gave each of his creditors a series of postdated checks to back up his promises. *Legally, no creditor can refuse to take a payment—even a small payment—each month, then go to court to sue you.* Once you've made such a plan, stick to it. Live by it and refuse to allow new debts to build up.

Another method for taking care of past-due bills is loan consolidation. If your bank manager knows you and trusts your word, you may be able to arrange a loan with him to pay off all your debts and then repay the bank loan with the 20 percent of your income that is available for debt reduction.

Don't make the mistake of thinking that the 10-70-20 plan won't work for you. It will work for anyone who is willing to try. If you obey these rules, you will become a good steward of what God entrusts to you and you will also build an estate for yourself and your loved ones.

Where There Is Vision There Is Provision

Proper management of money is important for you and your family's well-being. But there is another reason for getting your financial house in order. Many experts predict that our country—indeed, the world—is heading for financial disaster. Many of them predict that in the near future the United States will go through the most severe money crisis our nation has ever known.

There are several suggestions you can follow in order to be prepared for this possibility. First, you should have at least six months' income in savings. I know you may say this is impossible because you're just getting by now. But be realistic. *If times get really tough, you'll be forced to live on a fraction of what you're getting now.* So it would be much better to save now than to suffer later. You would need at least six months of income to help relocate in the event you lose your job because of an economic depression or because of persecution.

You should learn a craft where you could become self-employed during your crisis. If things get tough, many highly skilled workers as well as common laborers will be laid off. What then? It would be good to know how to work with your hands in a craft that would be in demand. Mechanics, farming, and shoe repair will always be needed. I know this may sound funny to the skeptic, but the next time you're in a large city and see tens of thousands of people on the streets, remember that a financial crisis could turn many of them into food beggars in a short time.

Will Rogers once said, "Land is a good investment because they aren't making any more of it." I recommend that you consider investing in a small piece of productive land away from metropolitan areas. For years I have cautioned Christians against purchasing expensive cars that depreciate from $85 to $100 a month sitting in the driveway. You can easily get by with an older car in good condition. This would save as much as $2000 to $3000 that would make a substantial payment on a piece of land by a spring, river, or lake in some remote place.

The reason your retreat should be a great distance from a large city is that in the event of a great financial disaster and a food panic, there will be many robberies and much food plundering in the metropolitan areas.

A concerned friend of mine said, "Lowell, it would be good if families would learn how to rough it—even if they only experimented on weekends. They need to learn how to cook on an open fire, how to use kerosene lanterns, and how to eat simple provisions. The day may come when that experience will be invaluable."

It's All Up to You

Whenever you approach an unknown situation there are two ways to respond. First, you can laugh and deny that it will ever happen. God knows we don't want it to happen, but what have you got to lose by being prepared? With a limited amount of conservation and preparation, you can protect yourself against an uncertain future.

The second thing you can do is to overreact and run around scared, with a doomsday mentality. Jesus told the wise servant to be faithful. Don't waste what God has given you, and at the same time don't fear or fret about the future.

I believe that many people will live to regret the way they waste their money on high-priced cars, homes, furniture, fancy foods, and sporting equipment. Most people would be better off buying only necessities and not so many luxuries. Work out a family budget and watch where your money is being spent. Some families in cities get together and create food co-ops where they're able to purchase food at near-wholesale prices. Food is a terribly expensive item today.

Cut out expensive habits of the flesh. A man who smokes two packs of cigarettes a day will spend over $300 a year for his habit. If he saves his money at 5-percent interest, in 40 years he will save enough to purchase a $36,000 home. And there are many homes where both husband and wife smoke. If they quit when they're 20, in 40 years they will have enough to purchase a $72,000 luxury home! That's a lot of expensive smoke! And think about this: if a husband and wife drink four to six packs of beer a week, they will drink up over $75,000 during their married life!

If you want to save money right now, cigarettes and alcohol may be keeping you broke. If you quit these habits you will save a fortune and feel better at the same time.

Managing money properly is an important natural law for success and prosperity. This one discipline alone has meant the difference between success and failure for thousands of people.

You can do it too. Coupled with the other natural and spiritual laws discussed in this book, wise money management can help you discover and enjoy *supernatural prosperity.*

Chapter 6
HOW TO PROSPER WITH THE OWNER OF EVERYTHING

If you understand and use the four natural laws which we have discussed so far, you will prosper even if you aren't a Christian and even if you don't believe in God. The four natural laws—managing your relationships, your mind, your time, and your money—will take you far down the road to success.

But to be *supernaturally prosperous*—to have *more* than money and wealth, and to be prosperous in spirit, mind, and body, you must also follow God's *spiritual* laws for prosperity. There are two sides to every coin, and there are two sides to supernatural prosperity. Both sets of laws must be observed in order to achieve the fullness of what God has for you. You may be spiritually prosperous without applying the natural laws, or you may be materially prosperous without applying the spiritual laws. But to be *supernaturally* prosperous, to enjoy all that God has for you in every area of your life, you must apply both sets of laws.

God Owns Everything

The first spiritual law for success and prosperity is—*you must recognize that God owns everything!* A Christian doesn't own anything—he only manages money for God.

Howard Hughes was a billionaire. When he died, someone asked how much he left. The answer was, "All of it." Here was a billionaire who died naked, swatting flies.

In the ultimate sense you don't own anything. You don't own houses or land, for as soon as you die you leave it all.

You don't even own your children. Your youngsters pass through you, but they are not of you.

You don't own your body—it goes back to the dust.

You don't own your spirit—it goes back to God at your death.

You don't own your soul—it belongs to God. God says "All souls are Mine."

So what do you own? Only one thing in the entire universe—your will. *It is your sole possession in life.* You can say "yes" or "no"; you can make choices on the direction you will go.

So the first spiritual law which helps form the foundation for financial freedom in your life is to recognize that *God owns everything.* You may possess certain things, but mere possession is not ownership. Time after time in His Word God affirms this truth:

"The earth is the Lord's, and the fullness thereof; the world, and they that dwell therein" (Psalm 24:1).

"The silver is mine, and the gold is mine, saith the Lord of hosts" (Haggai 2:8).

"Every beast of the forest is mine, and the cattle upon a thousand hills . . . and the wild beasts of the field are mine" (Psalm 50:10, 11).

Remember, *you may possess*, *but God owns*. You may earn, but it is God who enables you to earn: "Thou shalt remember the Lord thy God, for it is He that giveth thee power to get wealth" (Dueteronomy 8:18).

There is no such thing as a self-made man. There is only a man who refuses to recognize the power of God's hand in his life. You may think of some person who is not a Christian, who has never recognized God or given anything to God and yet appears to be successful. But I say that this person has nevertheless been enabled by God to earn everything he has. For it is in God that we "live, move, and have our being" (Acts 17:28). Furthermore, people who are financially successful have become so by applying God's principles, perhaps without knowing it.

Our Reasonable Service

The Apostle Paul wrote, "I beseech you therefore, brethren, by the mercies of God, that you present your bodies a living sacrifice, holy, acceptable unto God, which is your reasonable service" (Romans 12:1).

Therefore, we should dedicate to God all that we are, all that we have, and all that we shall ever be. And what does Paul say about this kind of complete dedication? It is your "reasonable service."

Such commitment is *reasonable* service on our part—not extreme fanaticism—because we belong to God. "It is He that hath made us, and not we ourselves; we are His people, and the sheep of His pasture" (Psalm 100:3). Don't you know that "you are not your own? For you are bought with a price; therefore glorify God in your body, and in your spirit, which are God's" (1 Corinthians 6:19, 20).

You are God's, so all you have belongs to God. You simply manage your possessions for Him.

A growing number of Christians are turning their businesses over to God. They take out just enough to make a decent living for their families, and the rest of the profit belongs to God's work. When everything you have belongs to God, it certainly takes the pressure off.

For instance, if you're a farmer and your farm belongs to God, when it doesn't rain you don't have to worry about it. You can say, "Lord, you've got a problem! It's not raining, and unless you send some rain, your crop is going to dry out!" That's a lot better than sitting there at night wondering and worrying about it yourself!

Some of the Crop

Now I want you to look at one of the most exciting passages of Scripture in all of the New Testament. Paul, writing to the church at Corinth, said: "Who goes to warfare at his own expense? Who plants a vineyard and does not eat of its fruit, or who finds a flock and does not drink of the milk of the flock? Do I say these things as a man, or does not the law say the same also? For it is written in the law of Moses, "Thou shalt not muzzle the mouth of the ox that treadeth out the corn. Is God concerned for the oxen, or does He say this for our sakes? For our sakes, no doubt, this is written" (1 Corinthians 9:7-10).

You see, Paul realized that although every thing in the universe belongs to God, the Lord allows us to keep some of everything which we take care of for Him. What soldier in the army has to pay his own expenses? And have you ever heard of a farmer who harvested his crop and didn't have the right to eat some of it? What shepherd in charge of a flock of sheep isn't allowed to drink some of the milk?

God Wants You to Have Plenty

Most of us seem to have trouble with this at one time or another. The writer of Proverbs noted, "There is that which scatters and yet increases, and there is that which withholds more than is suitable, but it tends to poverty" (Proverbs 11:24). Notice that God doesn't command us to be poor—He wants His children to withhold some of everything they get. The problem is *withholding more than is right.* God cautions us against being stingy with our giving.

Many of us worry about how to distribute what is ours and what is God's. We're so careful to keep plenty for ourselves and to measure exactly what goes to God.

How much better it would be if we understood God's divine law! When we realize that everything belongs to God anyway, and we turn it all over to Him, He will respond, "Since you're grinding this corn for Me, go ahead and eat all you want anytime you want to. Take all you need. If you're grinding it out, it's yours to have a mouthful anytime you want to."

Why Do the Wicked Prosper?

There's an old gospel song that expresses a problem many people have: "Tempted and tried, we're oft made to wonder why it should be thus all the day long, while there are others living about us, never molested though in the wrong."

Have you ever wondered why you're having such a hard time even though you're trying to do what is right? This is especially hard to understand when you look around and see ungodly people who seem to be prospering. They seem to be rich, happy, and coasting along luxuriously, while you work yourself to death just to keep your head above water. Do you know what I'm talking about?

This problem has been around for a long, long time. The prophet Asaph wrote, "I was envious at the foolish, when I saw the prosperity of the wicked" (Psalm 73:3).

Do you want to know why the wicked are rich today? The Bible gives a very simple answer. They are rich because they are holding the wealth God wants to give to His children. The Bible says, "A good man leaveth an inheritance to his children's children, and the *wealth of the sinner is laid up for the just*" (Proverbs 13:22).

Does that really mean what it sounds like? Let's look at some other verses and see if we can find confirmation of this concept.

Solomon, who was known as the wisest man who ever lived, wrote, "For God giveth to a man that is good in His sight wisdom and knowledge and joy; but to the sinner He giveth travail, to gather and to heap up, that he may have to him that is good before God" (Ecclesiastes 2:26).

Job said that the wicked man would not

always enjoy the prosperity he seemed to have in abundance: "Though he heap up silver as the dust, and prepare garments as the clay, he may prepare it, but the just shall put it on, and the innocent shall divide the silver" (Job 27:16).

So don't worry about the wealth and prosperity of unbelievers. That is money which God has in His savings account for His people. It all belongs to Him.

The Purpose of Prosperity

God teaches us that we should not love money, or hoard it, or covet it, but that we should use money as a means to send forth the gospel of Jesus Christ.

Have you entered into the highest motive for making money? Jesus said, "Seek ye first the kingdom of God, and His righteousness, and all these things shall be added unto you" (Matthew 6:33). Our primary concern should be the welfare of God's kingdom.

There are three truths to remember. First, all wealth belongs to God. Second, the ability to gain wealth is God's gift to us. And third, we should seek to use money to extend the kingdom of God on the earth. As we govern our actions by these guidelines, we will be well on the way to enjoying supernatural prosperity in our own lives.

Chapter 7
HOW TO FIND THE SOURCE OF SUPERNATURAL WEALTH

The second great spiritual law for success is that you must establish once-and-for-all who is your Source.

The Apostle James said, "Do not err, my beloved brethren. Every good gift and every perfect gift is from above, and cometh down from the Father" (James 1:16, 17). James was saying, "Don't make any mistake about it—God is your Source of all good things!"

The Source and the Messenger Boy

Have you heard the story of the Christian family that was going through a time of financial hardship? They had used up everything they had, and didn't even know where their next meal was coming from. The father and mother got down on their knees and cried out to God, asking Him to send in food so their children would not go hungry.

An unbeliever walking by their house overheard their prayer and decided to play a trick on them. He bought a huge box of groceries and put it on their front porch. He banged on the door, then ran away to see what would happen. When the Christian people opened the door and saw the groceries, they began to praise God for supplying the food.

Then the unbeliever walked up and said, "Why are you thanking God for those groceries? I'm the one who brought them to you."

The Christian father replied, "Oh, no—God answered our prayer and provided the groceries. But we do appreciate your being His delivery boy and bringing them to us."

Some people make the mistake of thinking that their job provides their income and is their source of supply. They need to realize that God is the Source and that the man's name on their paycheck and the corporation they work for are instruments which God uses to let the funds flow to them.

The Bible says, "My God shall supply all your needs according to His riches" (Philippians 4:19). Notice that the Scripture says "My God"—not the boss of the company you work for, nor your banker, nor the government. *God* is your Source.

Take Care of Your Tools

If you're going to experience prosperity, you

must realize that you can't run roughshod over the instrument that God uses to provide for your needs. A good craftsman always takes good care of his tools. So you are to take care of your job, or whatever other instrument God is using to supply your needs. But you must never lose sight of the fact that *God is the Source.*

"For promotion cometh neither from the east nor from the west nor from the south. But God is the Judge: He putteth down one and setteth up another" (Psalm 75:6,7). The Lord uses men as instruments to bring the wealth and prosperity He has planned for His saints. I'm sure you're familiar with Luke 6:38, which says, "Give, and it shall be given unto you." But too many people fail to read the entire verse. The last part of that verse says that an *abundance* of good things *"shall men give into your bosom."*

So remember that God is your Source and that everyone else is His instrument. Continuously expect a blessing from God. Remember that problems are doors through which Jesus can enter your life. *Needs are opportunities for God to enrich you.* If you have a pair of shoes that are about to wear out, you have a potential blessing on your hands if you handle it right. Every need is a door for God to minister to you.

The Key to Unlimited Power

One of the most beautiful lessons in the Bible is the story of Moses and the burning bush. You remember that Moses had been out in the desert for 40 years tending sheep. He saw a bush on fire and was drawn to it in fascination. He soon discovered that he was in the very presence of God. In that dramatic confrontation, Moses received his call to deliver the children of Israel from Egypt's bondage. With his divine calling, he received the key to drawing upon God's unlimited power.

God asked Moses, "What is that in your hand?"

Moses replied, "It's just a rod—my shepherd's staff."

God said, "Throw it down."

Moses might have reacted to this strange request in a very human way. He might have said, "Lord, don't make me give up my shepherd's staff. It's all I've got. It's my security. It's what I lean on. I use it to make my living tending the sheep."

The Results of Obedience

But Moses obeyed God's command to throw the rod down. When he did, it became a snake. It was instantly transformed into a living, moving, miraculous token of God's divine and unlimited power.

When the rod became a serpent, the Bible says that Moses ran from it. Don't make fun of Moses! You probably would have run too. How many times has God tried to demonstrate His miracle power in your life, but you backed away from it as far as you could? When God has tried to demonstrate that He is the Source of everything in your life, perhaps you've run off and shut your eyes and said, "Oh, no, I won't look. That scares me!"

God said to Moses, "Quit running and pick up that snake by the tail."

I don't know much about snakes, but I do know that if you're going to pick up a snake you don't grab it by the tail. You get it behind the head so that it can't turn around and bite you.

But God told Moses to pick up the serpent by the tail. When he obeyed, the serpent was transformed again into a rod—not just *any* rod, but the rod of God.

And it was that very rod that Moses used to work miracles before Pharoah. It was the rod of God that struck a rock and caused water to pour forth. It was the rod of God that was stretched over the sea and caused the waters to roll back.

When a stuttering shepherd from the desert discovered that God was his Source, he was able to stand up before a world dictator and command him, "Let God's people go!"

What Do You Have in Your Hand?

Can you imagine what could happen in your life if you started talking about God's job, God's car, God's house, God's children, God's money? It could transform you and let you realize how much is at your disposal as a child of God. What do you have in your hand today? Are you willing to throw it down and pick up the rod of God?

Consider the treasures of life that God has already bestowed upon you. Would you trade your eyesight for a million dollars? Or your hearing? Or even your sense of taste?

What is your health worth? What dollar value can you place on your sound mind? What about the treasures of food, or of having a home to live in?

Wonderful as all these things are, none of them can compare to the gift of God—Jesus Christ our Lord and Savior. He is the Source of all good gifts, and we are more than millionaires already in the good things He has given us.

There is no limit to what we can accomplish if we go out as managers and stewards of God's resources. But we must always remember that God is our Source of all supernatural wealth.

You Can Have Prosperity Power

Moses learned his lesson well. Years after his dramatic experience with God at the burning bush, we find him warning the children of Israel never to forget that God is their Source. He urged them never to say in their heart, "My power and the might of my hand hath gotten me this wealth. But thou shalt remember the Lord thy God, for it is He that giveth thee power to get wealth, that He may establish His covenant which He swore unto thy fathers, as it is this day" (Deuteronomy 8:17, 18). Isn't that a tremendous statement? Remember the Lord, for He is the One who gives you power to get wealth. He is your Source.

If you desire wealth as a means to extend the kingdom of God, the Lord will give you power to get wealth. God actually blesses you so that you can give more. And the more you give, the more you are blessed. Paul recognized this when he wrote, "God is able to make all grace abound toward you, so that, always having all sufficiency in all things, you may abound to every good work" (2 Corinthians 9:8). Paul was saying, "God, who is your Source, will make sure that you always have plenty so you can give to promote the kingdom of God and do good things for others."

Generous Giving, Generous Blessing

Paul also said, "He that soweth sparingly shall also reap sparingly, and he that soweth bountifully shall also reap bountifully" (2 Corinthians 9:6).

What does this mean in practical language?

Start practicing "seed giving" for every need you have, for every increase you want, for every venture you want to prosper in. If you have something that you want to turn out right, be sure to plant some seeds for it.

Giving is an essential part of recognizing God as your Source. Let's look at Proverbs 11:24, 25 again: "There is that which scatters, and yet increases, and there is that which withholds more than is suitable, but it tends to poverty. The generous soul shall be made fat, and he who waters shall be watered himself." These verses point out the important difference between the purely material approach to prosperity and the supernatural approach. The world says that we prosper by *gathering and increasing*, but God's Word says that we must *scatter* to increase.

God said that it is more blessed to give than to receive. Why? Because only what is *given* can be multiplied back to us. It is impossible for God to bless you if you hold back more than you should. *Giving is what triggers financial miracles! Nothing happens in God's prosperity program until someone gives something away.*

So after you have put all the natural laws for prosperity to work in your life, and acknowledge that God owns everything, *activate the Source of supernatural prosperity*. Get your eyes and attention off the instruments, or tools, through which blessings come, and focus them instead on your Source.

Chapter 8
HOW TO BANK ON GOD'S PROMISES

Several years ago, when evangelist Billy Graham began a great crusade in a stadium that had room for many thousands of people, he invited Roy Rogers and Dale Evans to be his special guests. When someone asked Roy and Dale if they thought the crusade would be a success, they replied, "Of course! It has to succeed because God doesn't sponsor any flops!"

I like that. God doesn't sponsor flops. The most important decision you can make in your entire life is to come under the personal management of the Lord. When God is your personal manager, you're going to prosper. You're going to win. You're going to succeed.

The question is, are you committed to Jesus Christ? Have you placed your life in His hands?

If you're struggling along in your own strength . . .

If you're tired of the hasslings of life . . .

If you're tired of poverty and want . . .

If you want to get a heavenly advantage . . .

Give your life to the Lord. Choose the right crowd. Concern yourself with the right concepts, and you will reap an abundant crop.

When we began this book I said that there are two sets of laws which must be obeyed if we are to enjoy supernatural prosperity. I outlined four natural laws regarding your relationships, your time, your thinking, and your use of resources. Then I covered three spiritual laws which involved our recognition of God's supremacy and the practical spiritual rules He has laid down for us to follow.

Steps to Supernatural Prosperity

Psalm 1 is based on this same formula. Verse 1 of the first Psalm deals with the natural laws: "Blessed [or happy] is the man that walketh not in the counsel of the ungodly, nor standeth in the way of sinners, nor sitteth in the seat of the scornful." Isn't it interesting how this one verse touches on how we spend our time, who we associate with, and what we feed our mind upon?

Now notice verse 2: "But his delight is in the law of the Lord, and in His law doth he meditate day and night." This verse certainly encompasses all the spiritual laws we have discussed in this book. I have always advised my family and the new converts I counsel with to always test against the Word of God any doctrine they've heard. Everything vital to our spiritual well-being is spelled out in detail in God's Word.

Having observed both the natural and the spiritual laws, what can we expect? Verse 3 provides the answer: "He shall be like a tree planted by the rivers of water, that bringeth forth its fruit in its season; his leaf also shall not wither, and whatsoever he doeth shall prosper."

What a fantastic promise! God says that if you choose the right friends, if you apply your mind to the right concepts, if you devote your time to worthwhile endeavors, if you acknowledge God and invest in His kingdom, you will reap an abundant crop. You can expect to be a winner.

God Loves a Winner

God receives no joy in seeing His children downtrodden, financially strapped, and flattened by defeat. God fashions no trophies for people who are constantly overrun by Satan in this world. He has no pleasure in seeing them constantly defeated by the enemy. The Lord gave us tremendous power over Satan. He wants us to use the victory weapons He forged at Calvary. His heavenly prizes aren't for those Christians who insist on living behind Satan's eight ball because of their neglect of His victory provisions. These trophies are for His *winners.*

"To him that overcometh will I give to eat of the tree of life, which is in the midst of the paradise of God. . . . To him that overcometh will I give to eat of the hidden manna, and will give him a white stone, and in the stone a new name written" (Revelation 2:7, 17).

At least four or five more times in the second and third chapters of Revelation God promises rewards to him who overcomes. And *you can overcome* if you use the resources God has already placed at your disposal. Don't be like the people to whom James said, "You have not because you ask not" (James 4:2).

Remember, poverty does not add to a man's influence. There are certain religious sects in the world that take an oath of poverty and swear themselves to a lifetime of poverty. There is absolutely nothing in God's Word that says that such a course of action will bring about any degree of respect from God or men. In fact, the Bible teaches just the opposite. You can go through the Bible and see example after example of the great men of faith who were described as having great assets and much material wealth.

Poverty Is a Negative Witness

Ecclesiastes 9:14, 15 tells a bitter story: "There was a little city, and few men within it; and there came a great king against it, and besieged it, and built great bulwarks against it. Now there was found in it a poor wise man, and he by his wisdom delivered the city; yet no man remembered that same poor man."

Do you think your poverty and lack of riches earns you respect in the eyes of your fellowman? *Think again.* This story shows that even though a poor man was able to deliver an entire city, after the battle was over no one paid him the slightest bit of attention. In fact, Solomon observes, "Nevertheless the poor man's wisdom is despised, and his words are not heard" (Ecclesiastes 9:16).

The Kingdom Key to Prosperity

The kingdom key to prosperity is found in Jesus' words in Matthew 6:33—"Seek ye first the kingdom of God and His righteousness, and all these things shall be added unto you." Jesus was saying, "Concentrate your heart, mind, and soul on the extension of God's kingdom, and then God will prosper you by giving you everything you need." If you build for God, God will build for you.

Jim Elliott died in 1955 in a jungle in South America. On the day of his death he wrote in his diary, "He is no fool who gives what he cannot keep to gain what he cannot lose." What a tremendous expression of faith in the promises of God! I tell you, God's promises are true. They are like money in the bank. You can depend on God's Word.

So if you want to become supernaturally prosperous, observe the natural laws we discussed earlier in this book. Those laws alone will transform your world and bring financial prosperity and success to you.

But go further than that. Seek to obey the *spiritual* laws also. They too have the power to bring great riches into your life. By combining the natural and the spiritual laws, you will find yourself enjoying a surging, flooding, overflowing rush of supernatural prosperity. You will find yourself realizing the blessings prayed for by

John when he said, "Beloved, I wish above all things that thou mayest prosper and be in health, even as thy soul prospereth" (3 John 2). And every promise of God's Word will be yours.

Count on God's Word

You can count on God's Word. "There hath not failed one word of all his good promise" (1 Kings 8:56). Step out on the promises of God and release a flow of supernatural prosperity into your life. Start enjoying the good things God wants to give you.

Expect happiness to flood your life. In fact, you can go ahead and start smiling now, for "the blessing of the Lord maketh rich, and He addeth no sorrow with it" (Proverbs 10:22).

This is the beginning of a whole new way of life for you. You may not make the entire transformation overnight, but don't get discouraged. Keep applying the principles I've outlined for you. Keep trusting God as your Source. Believe in His promises. They are as good as money in the bank.

So you can't fail. Supernatural prosperity is coming to you—it's already on the way. You are bound to succeed because God is your Sponsor.

And God doesn't sponsor any flops.

TO CONTACT THE AUTHOR, WRITE:

Lowell Lundstrom
Sisseton, South Dakota 57262